Materials, Materials, Materials

Plastic

Chris Oxlade

Heinemann Library
Chicago, Illinois

Designed by Storeybooks
Originated by Ambassador Litho Ltd.
Printed in Hong Kong / China

05 04 03 02 01
10 9 8 7 6 5 4 3 2 1

Library of Congress Cataloging-in-Publication Data

Oxlade, Chris.
   Plastic / by Chris Oxlade.
      p. cm. -- (Materials, materials, materials)
Includes bibliographical references and index.
   ISBN 1-58810-157-6
   1. Plastics--Juvenile literature. [1. Plastics.] I. Title. II.
Series.
TP1125 .O85 2001
668.4--dc21
                                        00-012893

Acknowledgments
The author and publishers are grateful to the following for permission to reproduce copyright material:
Corbis/Bob Krist, p. 4; Tudor Photography, pp. 5, 6, 7, 8, 9, 10, 13, 18, 20, 23, 25; Image Bank, p. 11; Stone, p. 12;
Photodisc, p. 14; PPL Library, p. 15; Kate Bryant-Mole, p. 16; Shell Library, pp. 17, 22; Barnaby's Picture
Library/H. K. Maitland, p. 19; Corbis, p. 24; Oxford Scientific Films/Edward Parker, p. 26; Science Photo Library,
p. 27; Noel Whittal, p. 29.

Cover photograph reproduced with permission of Tudor Photography.

Every effort has been made to contact copyright holders of any material reproduced in this book.
Any omissions will be rectified in subsequent printings if notice is given to the publisher.

Note to the Reader
Some words are shown in bold, **like this.**
You can find out what they mean by looking in the glossary.

Contents

What Is Plastic?

Plastic is made from **chemicals.** It is not a **natural** material. These plastic beads have just been made. They will be used to make other plastic things.

Plastic is an important material. People make many things from it. All the things in this picture are made of plastic.

Hard and Soft

Some plastics are very hard and **brittle.** It is not easy to stretch or bend them. When hard plastics are bent, they may snap in half.

Some plastics are very soft. They are easy to stretch or bend. Soft plastic does not go back into shape after it is stretched.

Hot and Cold

Some plastics become soft when they are heated. They become hard again when they cool down. They are called thermoplastics.

Other plastics do not become soft when they are heated. They stay hard. They are called thermosetting plastics.

Waterproof Plastics

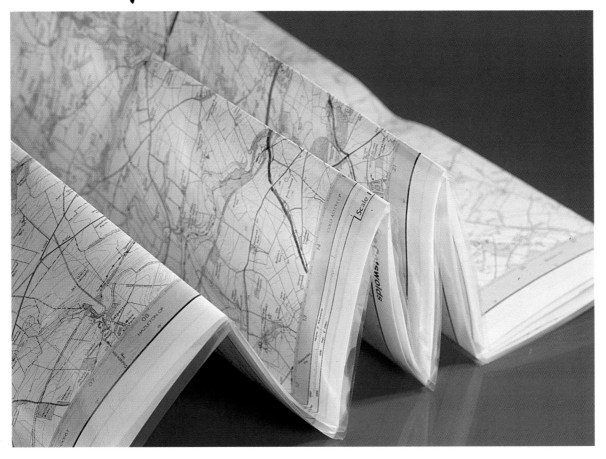

All kinds of plastic are **waterproof.** They do not let water soak into them. You can make paper waterproof by **laminating** it with plastic. The map in this picture has been laminated.

Because plastics are waterproof, they last for a very long time. They do not **rot** like wood. They do not **rust** like **steel,** even if they are left outside. This slide is made of plastic.

Electricity and Heat

Plastics do not let **electricity** pass through them. They are called electrical **insulators.**

Electric wires are covered in plastic. This keeps the electricity in each wire from flowing to other wires.

Some drinking cups are made from plastic. It does not let heat pass through it. It can keep hot drinks from burning a person's hands.

Making Plastics

Plastics are made from **chemicals.**
Many of the chemicals come from **oil**
found underground or under the ocean
floor. Different plastics are made by
mixing different chemicals together.

The material used to make this boat is called **fiberglass.** It is made by mixing **liquid** plastic with liquid glass. Fiberglass becomes hard a few minutes after it is put in place.

Shaping Plastics

Many plastic things are made in **molds.**
Hot, **liquid** plastic is poured into the mold
to harden. After it cools, the new thing is
taken out of the mold.

Long, thin plastic objects are made by pushing hot, liquid plastic through a hole. Plastic pipes and **fibers** are made this way.

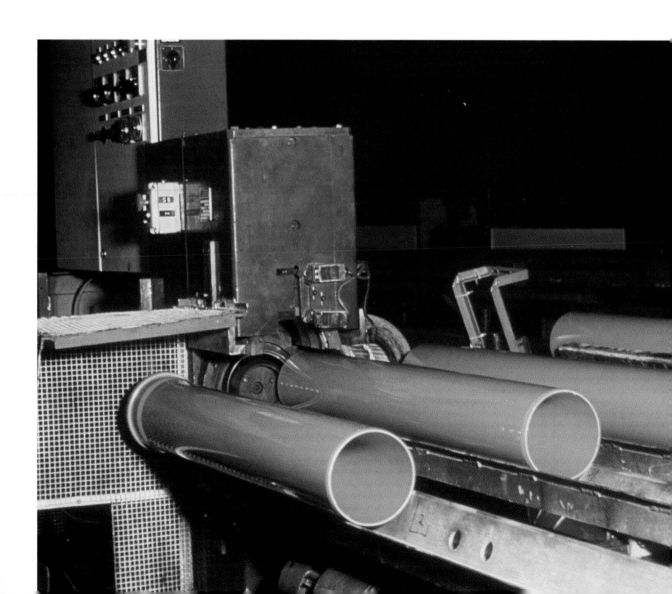

Bottles and Pipes

Plastic is useful for holding **liquids.** Plastic is often used instead of glass for making bottles. Plastic bottles do not break easily, and they do not weigh very much.

Plastic pipes carry liquids and gases. These strong, plastic pipes are being laid underground. They carry gas for cooking and heating. The plastic pipes will last longer than metal pipes would.

Plastic Packaging

Thin sheets of plastic are used to make bags and to wrap foods. Plastic can be wrapped around something and then heated. The plastic shrinks and seals the package.

Polystyrene is a very light kind of plastic. It is full of tiny air bubbles. Polystyrene is often used inside packages. It helps keep things from breaking in the mail.

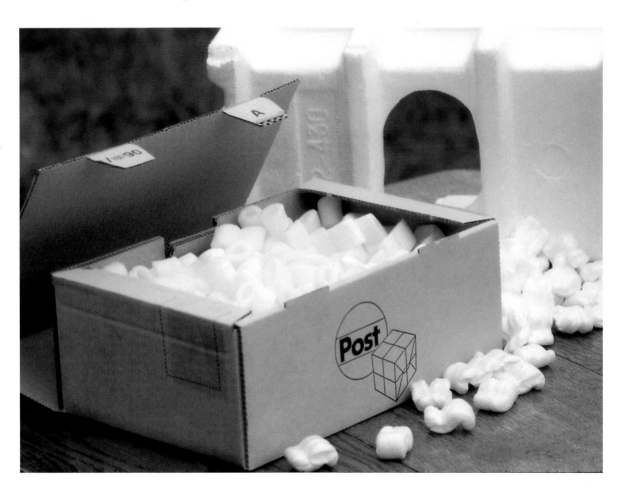

Fibers and Fabrics

A **fiber** is a long, thin string of material.
The fibers in this picture are made of a
plastic called nylon. Nylon is a plastic
that stretches easily.

A **fabric** is made by **weaving** fibers together. Fabrics like the one used to make this jacket are made with plastic fibers. They last longer than other fabrics.

Building with Plastic

Builders often use plastics. The windows
in this hockey stadium are made of hard,
see-through plastic. They will not shatter,
even if a player runs into them.

Window frames, **gutters,** and pipes
often are made from a plastic called PVC.
This plastic lasts a long time. It is strong,
and it is **waterproof.**

Recycling Plastic

Plastic is a useful material because it does not **rot.** But this also causes a problem. When we throw away plastic, it takes a long time to break down. That creates a lot of extra trash.

Some kinds of plastic can be **recycled.**
You can help gather plastic and place it in
special bins. The plastic is melted down to
make plastic beads. Then the beads are
made into new plastic things.

Fact File

▶ Plastic is made from **chemicals.** It is not a **natural** material.

▶ Some kinds of plastic are hard and not easy to stretch. Other kinds of plastic are soft and easy to stretch.

▶ Some kinds of plastic become soft when they are heated. Other kinds of plastic stay hard when they are heated.

▶ Plastics are **waterproof.** They do not **rot** or **rust.**

▶ **Electricity** and heat do not flow through plastics. Plastic is an **insulator.**

▶ Plastics are not attracted by **magnets.**

▶ Some kinds of plastic can be **recycled. Polystyrene** is hard to recycle.

Can You Believe It?

A plastic called Kevlar is five times stronger than **steel,** but weighs less. You could hang from a Kevlar **fiber** as thin as the lead in a pencil! This person is hanging from Kevlar fibers.

Glossary

brittle breaks or cracks easily

chemical material used to clean and protect something

electricity form of power that can light lamps, heat houses, and make things work

fabric knitted or woven material used for clothing and other coverings

fiber very thin thread or small piece of material as thin as one of your hairs

fiberglass strong material made from mixing plastic with glass threads

gutter low area made to carry water away from the surface of a roof

insulator material that does not let electricity or heat flow through it

laminate to seal plastic onto paper using heat

liquid something that flows, such as water or oil

magnet piece of iron or steel that pulls iron and steel things toward it

mold space into which liquid material is poured in order to form it

natural comes from plants, animals, or rocks in the earth

oil thick, black liquid found underground

polystyrene light plastic with lots of air bubbles in it, used to insulate or as a packing material

recycle to use a material again, often to make new things

rot to fall apart because of dampness

rust to turn into a reddish-brown, brittle material that forms on iron or steel when it is left in contact with moist air

steel strong metal made mostly from iron

waterproof does not let water in or out

weave to make fabric by putting strings of material over and under each other

More Books to Read

Gibbons, Gail. *Recycle!: A Handbook for Kids.* New York: Little, Brown & Co., 1996.

Madgwick, Wendy. *Super Materials.* Austin, Tex.: Raintree Steck-Vaughn, 1999.

Warbrick, Sarah. *What Is See-Through?* Chicago: Heinemann Library, 1998.

Index